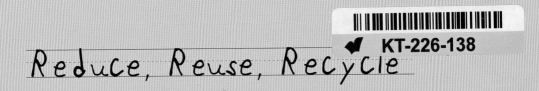

Reduce, Reuse, Recycle

Paper

Alexandra Fix

Heinemann
LIBRARY

www.heinemann.co.uk/library
Visit our website to find out more information about **Heinemann Library** books.

To order:

☎ Phone ++44 (0)1865 888066

▤ Send a fax to ++44 (0)1865 314091

▢ Visit the Heinemann Bookshop at www.heinemann.co.uk/library to browse our catalogue and order online.

First published in Great Britain by Heinemann Library,
Halley Court, Jordan Hill, Oxford OX2 8EJ, part of
Harcourt Education.
Heinemann is a registered trademark of Harcourt
Education Ltd.

Editorial: Cassie Mayer and Diyan Leake
Design: Steven Mead and Debbie Oatley
Picture research: Ruth Blair
Production: Duncan Gilbert

Origination: Chroma Graphics (Overseas) Pte Ltd
Printed and bound in China by South China
Printing Company Ltd

ISBN 978 0 431 90757 4
12 11 10 09 08

10 9 8 7 6 5 4 3 2 1

British Library Cataloguing in Publication Data
Fix, Alexandra, 1950-
    Paper. - (Reduce, reuse, recycle)
    1. Waste paper - Juvenile literature 2. Waste paper -
    Recycling - Juvenile literature 3. Waste minimization -
    Juvenile literature
    I. Title
    363.7'288

Acknowledgements
The publishers would like to thank the following for
permission to reproduce photographs: Alamy pp. **5**
(David Wootton), **6** (Directphoto), **8** (Philip Scalia), **12**
(Chris Howes/Wild Places Photography), **16** (John T.
Fowler), **23** (David R. Frazier Photolibrary), **25** (Neil
Cooper); Corbis pp. **4**, **7** (Kim Kullish), **9** (Philip Gould),
10 (Frank Lukasseck/Zefa), **11** (Gary Braasch), **13** (Sygma/
Langevin Jaques), **15** (Peter Morgan/Reuters), **17** (Jose
Luis Pelaez, Inc.), **18** (Paul Almasy), **19** (Jose Luis Pelaez,
Inc.), **20** (Karl Weatherly), **21** (Craig Hammell), **22**
(Herbert Kehrer/Zefa), **26**, **27** (Jim Winkley/Ecoscene);
Harcourt Index p. **14**; Harcourt Education p. **29** (Tudor
Photography); Science Photo Library p. **24** (Sheila Terry).

Cover photograph reproduced with permission of Corbis
(Royalty Free).

The publishers would like to thank Simon Miller for his
assistance in the preparation of this book.

Every effort has been made to contact copyright holders
of any material reproduced in this book. Any omissions
will be rectified in subsequent printings if notice is given to
the publishers.

Contents

What is paper waste?...4

What is made of paper?..6

Where does paper come from?..................................8

Will we always have paper?......................................10

What happens when we waste paper?....................12

How can we reduce paper waste?...........................14

How can we reuse paper?...16

How can we recycle paper?......................................18

Where can we take paper for recycling?...............20

How is paper recycled?..22

How do we use recycled paper?.............................24

How can you take action?..26

Make a papier mâché bowl......................................28

Glossary..30

Find out more..31

Index...32

Some words are shown in bold, **like this**. You can find out what they mean by looking in the glossary.

What is paper waste?

Every day we use paper. We write on notebook paper, read books, and use other paper items. Paper is an important material, but sometimes it is wasted.

Paper is often wasted.

⟶

Paper waste piles up. ↑

Paper waste is paper that is thrown away. Most paper can be used again or **recycled**. This wastes less paper.

What is made of paper?

Many useful items are made of paper. Schools have paper items such as books, notebooks, computer paper, newspapers, and magazines.

Pupils use many paper items.

Office supply stores sell many different types of paper.

Many items from the supermarket come in paper packaging. There are paper napkins, cups, plates, egg boxes, and juice cartons.

Where does paper come from?

Paper is made from trees. To make paper, trees are cut down and the wood is cut into small pieces. These pieces are mixed with water and **chemicals** to make wood **pulp**.

Wood is also cut down to build houses. ↓

These are huge paper rolls at a factory.

Wood pulp is **bleached** white and dried into big sheets of paper. The sheets are made into large rolls. The paper rolls are cut, packaged, and sent to **factories** that make paper items.

Will we always have paper?

Trees are a **renewable resource**. We can grow more trees, but it takes many years for them to grow tall.

It has taken many, many years for these trees to grow so tall.

It is important to plant new trees when old trees are cut down.

Trees are important for the **environment**. If we reuse or **recycle** paper, fewer trees will have to be cut down.

What happens when we waste paper?

Paper waste is harmful to the **environment**. Paper and cardboard waste take up a quarter of the space at **landfill sites**. Landfills are where rubbish is buried.

Paper buried in landfills gives off a gas that can start fires. ⟶

Chemicals used at paper factories can get into nearby rivers. This can harm or kill fish and plants.

When we waste paper, more paper has to be made. Harmful **chemicals** are released into the air at paper **factories**. Chemicals can also get into soil.

How can we reduce paper waste?

Vegetables can be wrapped in reused paper.

We can reduce paper waste by using less paper. Use reusable cloths instead of kitchen paper. Use glass dishes instead of paper plates.

Try not to buy things with too much packaging. Check items before you buy them. Choose the ones that use least packaging.

Some toys come in cardboard boxes that can be **recycled**.

How can we reuse paper?

You can reduce paper waste by reusing paper. Write or draw on both sides of a sheet of paper. Use the clean side of scrap paper for printing out documents.

Give away old books to a library or charity shop.

Old newspaper can be used for art projects.

Reuse boxes, gift bags, and tissue paper when you give presents. Try wrapping gifts in scrap paper or magazines instead of buying new wrapping paper. You can make new gift tags by cutting up old greeting cards.

How can we recycle paper?

When paper is **recycled**, it is broken down and used again to make new paper. Most **communities** have a recycling programme for materials such as paper, plastic, and glass.

Many newspapers are printed on recycled paper.

Paper needs to be sorted carefully for recycling.

To get paper ready for recycling, keep the papers dry. Place papers of the same type together. Separate cardboard, newspaper, and white computer paper.

Where can we take paper for recycling?

Recycling lorries pick up items made out of paper, plastic, metal, and glass.

In some places, a lorry picks up **recycling** items from homes. Then they are taken to a recycling centre.

If your **community** does not have a recycling programme, you can take used paper to a recycling centre. From there it gets taken to a **factory** where it is made into recycled paper.

Paper must be sorted at a recycling centre.

How is paper recycled?

At a **recycling** centre, paper is separated into newspaper, white paper, and cardboard. It is then pressed into big bundles and taken to a paper **factory**.

These bundles of paper are ready to go to a paper factory.

This wood pulp will become new paper. ↑

Bundles are cut into pieces and mixed with hot water to form **pulp**. The pulp is then cleaned to remove ink, glue, and staples. Recycled pulp is added to new pulp to make paper.

How do we use recycled paper?

Many things are made from **recycled** paper. Some shops sell recycled paper items such as writing paper, drawing paper, tissues, and kitchen paper.

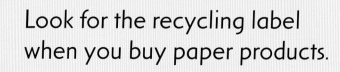

Look for the recycling label when you buy paper products.

Recycled paper, cardboard, and glue can be made into furniture. ↑

Plasterboard can also be made with recycled paper. Plasterboard is used to make walls in new homes.

How can you take action?

You can help reduce paper waste in your **community**. Ask family and friends to **recycle** paper. Use an old cardboard box to make a recycling box at home.

Put one paper recycling box in your bedroom and another in your kitchen. ↑

STIC, GLASS, CANS
TION CALL: 533-5353

Work together with friends on recycling projects at school.

Ask your teacher if your class can start reusing and recycling paper. If we all take part, we can reduce paper waste.

Make a papier mâché bowl

Ask an adult to help you with this project.

You will need:

- water
- flour
- permanent marker
- large bowl
- balloon (filled with air)
- empty yoghurt pot with lid
- strips of newspaper (about 4 cm wide by 10 cm long)

1. Mix two cups of flour and two cups of water in a large bowl.
2. Draw a line around the middle of your balloon. Put it in an empty container, knotted side down.
3. Dip the newspaper strips into the mixture. Lay the coated newspaper on to the balloon.
4. Continue to place coated newspaper strips over the surface of the balloon. Overlap each strip

28

Step 3   Step 7   Step 10

until everything below the line is covered. Then add a second layer of strips.

5. Put the balloon aside to dry overnight.

6. When the paper is dry, pop the balloon and remove it from your new bowl.

7. Turn the bowl upside down. Take the lid from the yoghurt pot and tape it on to the bottom. This will give your bowl a flat surface to rest on.

8. Cover the bottom with the coated strips of newspaper.

9. Put it aside to dry overnight.

10. Decorate your bowl with paints, collage materials, or anything you like.

Glossary

bleach   clean or whiten something using a chemical substance

chemical   basic element that makes up all things

community   group of people who live in one area

environment   natural surroundings for people, animals, and plants

factory   building or buildings where something is made

landfill site   large area where rubbish is dumped, crushed, and covered with soil

pulp   mixture of cut pieces of wood and water

recycle   break down a material and use it again to make a new product. Recycling is the act of breaking down a material and using it again.

renewable resource   something that can be replaced by nature

Find out more

Books to read

How We Use Materials: Paper, Anita Ganeri and Holly Wallace (Franklin Watts, 2006).

Using Materials: How We Use Paper, Chris Oxlade (Raintree, 2005).

Why Should I Recycle? Jen Green (Hodder Wayland, 2002).

Websites

Waste Watch work to teach people about reducing, reusing, and recycling waste. You can visit www.recyclezone.org.uk to find out more information about waste and to try some online activities.

Find out where you can recycle in your local area at: www.recyclenow.com by typing in your postcode. You can also find out more about which items can be recycled, more facts about waste, and what you can do to help!

Index

books **4, 6**
boxes **15, 17, 26**

cardboard **12, 19, 22, 26**
chemicals **13**
computer paper **6, 19**
cups **7**

drawing paper **24**

egg boxes **7**

factories **9, 13, 21, 22**

gift bags **17**
gift tags **17**
glass **14, 18**

juice cartons **7**

kitchen paper **24**

landfills sites **12**

magazines **6, 17**

napkins **7**
newspapers **6, 17, 19, 22**
notebooks **4, 6, 24**

packaging **7, 15**
paper waste **5, 12, 13, 14, 16, 26, 27**
plasterboard **25**
plastic **18**
plates **7**

recycling **19, 20–21**
renewable resources **10**

schools **6, 27**
scrap paper **16**
supermarkets **7**

tissue paper **17**
tissues **24**
trees **8, 10–11**

wood pulp **8–9, 23**
wrapping paper **17**
writing paper **24**